The Purple Door

A Spiritual Journey
Through Poetry and Prose

By: Shel Chrisco

For Clay,

who gave a silenced woman,

Strength

to speak:

to grow:

to love:

to write.

I love you more than words can say.

For as long as waters flow and fires burn.

Table of Contents

There once was a girl,

who found herself

in the woods....

The Window and the Moon

She often found herself
at the window in her room,
staring out into the night,
gazing at the moon.

There was something in the stillness,
something in the light
it kept her feeling safe and sound,
and chased away the fright.

It was as though the stars shone for her,
their twinkle in her eyes.
She dreamed she might reach out one night,
and touch them in the sky.

Though they were a million miles away,
they seemed the only friends who ever looked her way.

The Closet Fort

She tore everything out of her closet,
and there she built a hiding place
almost like the treetop branches
where she always felt so safe.

She brought all her notebooks,
and filled the pages with tales.
At night she'd lie there dreaming,
in the place she now knew so well.

The Quiet Place

The cold grass against her back
brought more comfort than anything else.
There, she could lie
and let the world fall away.

The kids at school found her strange —
while they ran and played in packs,
she tried to show them
how the earth could cradle a tired soul.

But they wanted none of it.

In the end,
she kept it all
to
herself.

Streetlights

She always hated when the streetlights flickered on.
She knew it was time to return to reality.
The woods' woven tales that drew her in
held tightly to her heart.

She often wondered if the forest felt her absence,
if it mourned her leaving each day.
She wondered if the woods would ever let her go
if she asked them not to.

And she wondered
if she would even care
if they didn't.

The Mask

She sat alone on the playground today.
She wondered, Would any friends want to play?
But the anxiety inside her mind
didn't allow her to ask
so she sat, all alone, building herself a mask.

She watched the others laugh with glee,
and whispered, Why can't that be me?
Then she realized, with that mask in place,
she could be anyone and never feel out of place.

So she strapped on that face and faked a grin,
ran up to the group and dove right in.
She said something silly; they all began to laugh.

Even though it was at her own expense,
she learned that day how to belong in the class.

Second Language

She was never the prettiest; not the smartest.
She had trouble getting out of her own way;
stumbled through life.

She learned that laughter could carry her,
so she mastered quick-witted humor.
Sarcasm became her second language;
she was never afraid to be the punchline.

Funny, the things humor can hide.

The Way She Was

She wanted to be liked for the way
she moved her hands excitedly
when something caught her attention;

for the way she cried while reading,
because the characters had become part of her world;

and for the way she laughed
at things you really shouldn't laugh about.

She wanted to be liked
for all the chaos
that made her who she was.

The Paper Friend

She spent her days in writing,
turning thoughts into rhyme.
She learned so soon to free her heart
when pen met paper; thoughts became lines.

Her thoughts escaped so quickly
her pen could barely keep up.
The page became her closest friend;
it listened, and never spoke up.

The Moon Girl

There was a girl that they all loved,
bright and beautiful as the moon.
They longed to fill her dreaming heart,
to be the melody in her tune.

Much like the moon, she waxed and waned;
at times she even eclipsed.
Forever shifting who she was,
yet none of them noticed it.

To them, she seemed forever the same,
her light each day reborn.
To them she was simply that radiant girl
whom everyone adored.

She tried to be who others needed her to be,
yet longed to stay the same.
Like the moon, she had no control ;
her light was meant to wane.

No one ever knew who she truly was;
they only loved the version they saw.
Never seeing that even in her darkest nights,
her beauty outshone them all.

Fire and Shadows

She's made of fire and sunlight,
burning brightly for the world to see,
but she prefers the shadows,
nestled deep among the trees.

Don't worry, she's not lonely there;
nothing in the dark's her foe.
She weaves through the midnight like a raven,
and pens her thoughts like Poe.

Reach for the Sun

Spending all that time in the woods
taught her many things about life, like this:

Tree branches reach slowly toward the sun.
It doesn't matter how vast the canopy above them
they bend and grow, up and around,
knowing only the warmth they need to survive.

We must all reach for the sun
no matter what shadows surround us.

Sun Child

Though she dances in the moon's waxing glow,
and harnesses its pull to run wild,
she still longs to wake in the warmth of morning —
for that girl will always be
a Sun Child.

Face to the Sun

It was hard to catch her eye.
Every time someone saw her,
she was walking with her face to the sun.

They wondered how she did it
how she walked that way,
never seeming to stumble or stray.

It was as if the sun guided her,
whispering what lay in her path,
so she'd never need
to look away.

…..they spoke to her,

the trees knew her name,

the wind embraced her,

the Sun called her his own,

the Moon held her secrets,

the Gods, celebrated…..

The Night's Embrace

The stars draw her out into the night,

twinkling high above the trees.

Her face tilts upward to the sky.

The chill in the air cannot subdue her;

the night embraces her warmly

as one of its own.

Safely Kept

The darkness never made her fearful;
the stars just guided her way.
She grew a little older
and a little bolder each day.

She crept out beneath the moonlight,
while the rest of the world still slept.
Lying in the grass, watching the stars
she always felt safely kept.

The Moon Called to Her

The moon called to her
like whispers along the branches
as wind shivered through the trees;
like the first hint of sun
flinting through cloud to break into dawn;
like dew crowning each blade of grass
before rushing down to meet the cold earth below.

The moon called to her
sending melodies of false dreams
strumming in tune with her soul;
sending tendrils of empty promises
dancing through the core of her heart;
sending darkness ebbing and flowing
through the sea of her being;
weaving doubts into her essence.

The moon called to her
"Run," it said,
"and I will be the one to catch you.
I will light your path ahead.
I will scatter the stars
to form your puzzle."

The moon called to her.
It beckoned her.
"Run."

Static Awakening

She spoke up to the sky,

certain someone might hear.

Her truth rang out loudly

no longer bound by fear.

There was no booming answer,

no voice that echoed her call,

but a hum rose from the earth below

a current beneath it all.

She felt it climb her body,

rooting deep within her soul.

For the first time in her existence,

she didn't feel alone.

She wasn't sure how awakening should be,

but she knew she'd come closer

to the brightest version

of "me."

The Wind Answered

She screamed for someone to hear her,
her face twisted, anxious and wild..
When no human voice returned her cry,
the wind whispered, I hear you, child.

The Strange Girl

The world felt different to her suddenly.
She wanted to show them
how she moved through it now
how it bent and breathed
to fit the rhythm of her life.

She wanted to tell them
how the air that stirred the grass
spoke in soft whispers of secrets untold.
She wanted them to see
that hugging trees was okay
that listening was enough.

But they whispered about her now.
She was the strange girl
who didn't fit in.
She was weird
and outcasted.

She found herself alone among them.
They found themselves afraid
around her.

Among the Authors

Each day she hid out in the library,

while the others gathered to chat.

She found herself at home with authors

Byron, Shakespeare, Poe, and Plath.

She'd eat her lunch in silence,

her nose buried deep in a book,

never giving the world around her

another single look.

The Path to the Trees

She sat through each class,

waiting for her moment to escape.

She knew one day she'd break free

and fly out of that place.

She couldn't wait to leave it behind

to breathe, to simply be,

to walk the winding path again

and find her way to the trees.

Goddess of the Trees

She walks in silence among the trees,
raindrops carried within the breeze.
Moisture gathers in her hair,
ringlets falling on skin so fair.

Leaves reach out, brushing her skin,
begging her to let them in
to share the secrets she keeps inside,
to free the fears she's learned to hide.

She dances beneath the dripping brush,
the forest around her falls to hush,
to watch her laughing, wild and free
her heart unbound, in pure release.

Blonde hair catching the sun's soft beams,
green eyes deeper than forest dreams.
She is one with leaf and tree —
she is a Goddess, for all to see.

They Called Her Witch

Time has a way of ticking by
even when we aren't looking.

Before she knew it,
she had grown darker, but not bitter.
Stronger but alone.

They whispered now about her
this angelic girl who had gone dark.
They called her weird, freak, goth.

They called her

Witch.

When She Became the Witch

She built a wall around her,

to keep the bad ones out.

Sometimes they'd still break through

and she would have to shout!

No one seemed too frightened

when she became a bitch.

Oh, but you should've seen them scatter

when she became the Witch.

Wings of Her Own

Her wings aren't white anymore,

but she doesn't seem to mind.

There are flowers in her hair,

and stars in her eyes.

.....she soon found herself

a Raven amongst

sheep.....

A Raven Heart

A raven heart,

a witchy soul

not meant to be understood,

not meant to be controlled.

The Creepy Kid

She painted her nails much darker;

her clothes followed suit.

She knew it only fed their whispers,

knew the rumors that would root.

She was the creepy kid in the hallway,

the girl no one seemed to like

but she didn't care what they thought anymore.

She was always ready for the fight.

The Labyrinth

Many tried to walk through the chaos of her mind
a labyrinth of twists and turns,
walls stretching high into the sky.

She weaved through it with quiet grace,
never losing her way,
yet never finding an end.

She wasn't sure
if it was a beautiful puzzle
or a waking dream
or just a nightmare.

Lost Literature

She is lost to this world —

her mind flitting from one book quote to the next,

her heart beating to the rhythm

of the next chapter that moved her.

Her face always tilted toward the sky,

searching for the index of life.

If you had to find her on a shelf,

she'd be with the lost literature —

each page dog-eared and worn,

words circled, margins whispered in,

her paper soft and brittle.

A book well-loved by some,

and misunderstood by others.

Reset

She was tired,

and her exhaustion stirred old anxieties.

It wasn't anything personal —

just her mind's way

of resetting the boundaries

she'd let fall away.

For a girl can only take so many jabs

before she finally jabs back —

with

silence.

Golden Silence

She is quiet

in moments when others are loud

not because she has nothing to say,

but because she carries too much

for deaf ears to hear.

If silence is golden,

then she is the brightest of leaves,

falling from autumn trees

in the stillest of moments.

The Windstorm

Sometimes the things she doesn't say

build until they whoosh out of her like a windstorm

blowing through to destroy

everything in their path.

There is no warning for her kind.

The Roar of Silence

How

horribly

deafening

the

roar

of

silence

can

be.

….. before long she found the isolation

Slipping her

into a deep depression,

into a deep hole of darkness …..

Suffocate

Sometimes when she tries to breathe,

the air just won't come.

Turning blue beneath the pressure

where is the pressure coming from?

The world feels so heavy,

it suffocates her.

Nowhere to turn,

no corner of the world.

Gasping for sweetness

air upon her lips

she falls back to earth;

even the ground dismisses.

Silent pleas rising

through tears that stream,

the fight is fleeing from her now

nothing left to redeem.

The Shadow

Darkness edged around her frame;
the feelings left were not the same.
Sometimes it seems that all is lost
isolation is the payment's cost.

She ripped the wings from her own back,
giving herself no grace, no slack.
Running in place, yet getting nowhere,
abusing her body without a care.

It's hard to be here when she longs to be there,
hidden behind, away from their stares.
Someone lies dying a few feet away
a shadowed form, on bleak display.

Its eyes are hollow, yet burn through her soul;
breaking her strength seems its only goal.
As the shape grows clear for the world to see,
she gasps aloud-
the shadow is me.

The Enchanted Laugh

Everyone wanted the girl
with the enchanted laugh
and so, she cried alone,
masking sorrow with rehearsed glee.

You wonder how long
someone can keep up a charade?

Years,
if need be.

Inside Her Mind

Wrapped up deep inside her mind,

hell has nothing worse, you'll find.

She tortures herself with all she's not

good enough, smart enough, pretty. just not.

Try as she might, she can't break the disdain,

living her life in self-inflicted pain.

Lips plaster smiles across her face,

eyes hide the weight of pure disgrace.

She grins through tears till they're appeased,

and when she's alone, her cheeks are streaked.

She runs to the woods, to hide in the trees —

finally still,

finally at peace.

The Angel Mask

Put together, so it seems
a smile upon her face.
An angel who shelters all she loves,
never fallen from grace.

She walks on clouds, she lives in dreams,
no worries in the world — or so it seems.
Yet they never see who she really is,
nor feel the ache her heart conceals.

The perception they get is what she exudes;
none of it true, all carefully used.
Behind those wings so white and pure
hides a darkness she must endure.

Demons perch upon her back,
tugging her like puppet strings.
A smile she wears to hide the ache,
to keep her world from caving in.

So very few will ever know
the truth she guards within.
So very few will reach her soul
enough for her to call them friend.

Where the Light Used to Be

Look within her and you'll see
the place where light once used to be.
Now shattered there, the glow steers clear
the quiet place she hides her fear.

An outer core that seems so strong,
a smile she wears to move along.
The tears stay hidden till none remain
she breaks, but never will explain.

To let one in would give away
the secrets she can't bear to say.
If they saw the damage deep inside,
they'd understand why others don't try

to break into her heart and soul,
no way to mend that gaping hole.

Darkness

Trying to stay busy with no one there,
Darkness calls, and tickles her hair.

"No one cares, but you see, I do.
Deep down inside, I know you care too."

When loneliness finally seeped its way in,
it didn't take long — Darkness became her friend.

It told her she needed no one but it;
Darkness stayed close as she silently sat.

It hugged her tightly, no warmth, no heat,
whispering promises it would never retreat.

She followed wherever the Darkness led,
did exactly whatever it said.

A beautiful girl now cloaked in black,
with Darkness clinging upon her back.

Tendrils wrapped around her core
no light touches her anymore.

The Dark Within

She's not the angel they all believe
there's darkness there they do not see.
Her eyes may shimmer in the sun,
but blackness waits, coming undone.

A glamour, if you will,
to hide what dwells inside;
some things in life
are better to hide.

She laughs with a light that fills her face,
yet watch the darkness will take its place.
A grimace in laughter, a smirk in her smile,
a glint that betrays her all the while.

The darkness is more her
than she is herself,
pushing the light
back onto the shelf.

And when she needs to cover the night,
trust she can switch on the light.
But cross her once, and you'll realize:
the shadow lives behind her eyes.

Running from Herself

Running from an unseen enemy,
she runs alone.
The earth's tears stream down her face,
leaving her hollow, more isolated still.
The breath of the world reaches for her,
pushing against her skin.
She pushes harder,
certain that at the other end of this place
there must be a blink of light.
Her feet dig deep into the ground below,
searching for leverage amid the turmoil within.
The burn of her soul pounds through her chest
as her breathing turns to gasps.
The silence around her deafens;
her feet pound out a rhythm of survival.
Then a glimmer, a blink of light through the leaves
a single spark of hope.
She fights through pain,
through the demons whispering she cannot go on.
Breaking through into sunlight,
she falls to the earth,
gasping, trembling
smiling as warmth beats against her skin.
She has reached the beginning.
And standing there before her
is the only enemy
she will ever truly know
the one she can never outrun:
herself.

Our Greatest Enemy

Sometimes a person can spend so long
walking in the darkness,
that they never stop to face
what caused it to begin.

Our greatest enemy
is often
ourselves.

…..once she realized that she must face herself,

and did, she grew,

spiritually, magically, and strongly

into a savage force to be reckoned with …..

Gray-Eyed Girl

Gray-eyed girl,
rotate the world.

Fly your path
on wings of black.

Set ablaze
all that dares to stand your way.
Let the flames rise high
reflected in your eyes,
burning behind your smile.

Let the heat melt the fields.
Let them see
what's real.

The Raging Witch

She wasn't the same.
Something inside her had cracked
left her with a cold longing
for the parts of herself she'd lost.

But somewhere along the way,
a tiny spark had kindled,
deep within the recesses of her soul
and like wildfire, it spread,
melting every trace of ice it found.

If they had shivered
beneath the Ice Witch's glare,
they would burn beneath
this Raging Witch's stare.

The witch with frost in her veins
had been indifferent, subdued
but this fire rising within her?
Oh no.
She was ready to pillage anything
in her path.

She was different now.

And they were all
going to understand
why.

Through the Fog

A heavy fog blanketed the land,
hiding the trees and the homes.

Though muted, the sun broke through the clouds,
still lighting the world around her.

She's like that, too
a beaming sun,
shining through the fog
at those who would try
to snuff her out.

New Mornings

She loves the way new mornings feel
when the world is still dark,
and the moon makes its quiet departure
to give way to the sun.

Much like her past,
fading
into a new start.

The Black Viola

She is a black viola
in a bed of morning glories
still standing tall,
long after
the morning glories
have faded
into night.

The Cage

She sat quietly in her cage,
singing her life away.
Watching clouds drift past the window,
day after day.

She wondered what it might feel like
to spread her wings and fly.

So, one day,
she threw open the door,
and stopped letting life
pass her by.

Wildfire

She is a wildfire,
raging high into the sky
leaving tree branches singed
in her wake.

Sure, they will grow back,
but the memory remains

the mark of where
she burned her name.

Friday the Thirteenth

She was different, that one
appearing every so often
in all her dark,
terrifying glory.

Hissing at passersby,
glaring at those
who dared to speak.

She beckoned them to run
perhaps even trip.

No, she was not like the other holidays.
No Christmas lights glittering for her.

She was **Friday the Thirteenth**
in human form
and she owned it.

Black Bird

You wouldn't understand
you simply cannot see.

I am a black bird,
and I was born to fly free.

Break my wings,
cage my soul
still, a black bird
I shall be.

This world may grasp and hold you tight,
but it nor you
can ever hold me.

The Skeleton Key

She'll unlock all your secret doors,
skeleton key in hand
fashioned from the bones
of those
who dared her to take a stand.

She'll grin as she slips inside,
the key tucked back in her bag.

They'll stare in shock,
completely confused

"Weren't all witches
supposed to look like hags?"

Darkest Night

Darkest night, blackest wings
soaring high above all earthly things.

Moon beaming bright, serene, and pale
she'll catch you in
her witch's spell.

…..One day in the midst of her journey,

she felt a shift; an electric current;

a magickal casting of energy.

She looked up

and there he stood…..

The Dark Angel

She saw him from across a crowded room.

Sure, it was the typical start
to most love stories
but this story wasn't like the others.

He was a dark angel,
tucked quietly into the corner,
believing no one saw him.

But that was impossible
he carried an energetic magnetism
that drew the room toward him.

They stared with longing, with envy.

She stared with wonder.

And for the rest of the night,
she saw nothing
but him.

The Old Soul

He was an old soul
speaking of lives never lived,
of days long gone.

He quoted poets,
built philosophies
from the words of those
who had already left this world.

All while sipping Scotch,
thinking out loud
of some new story
he might write someday.

He was the worn leather book
hidden on a back shelf
darkness etched in light.

He held secrets
unknown to those
who never took the time
to skim the pages.

He was worth quoting
in his own right.

He just didn't know it.

The Collision

It's not that her life wasn't moving before

she was a single soul

making her way through the world quietly,

alone, only half of herself.

Then suddenly,

there was another

walking a similar path,

loving similar things

and their worlds collided.

A beautiful symphony

two hearts

beating to the same tune,

two souls

finally finding

the half they'd been missing.

The Dark Green Witch

He saw through her mask
into the depths of her soul,
into the places she hid from the world.

He heard the things she didn't say,
felt the truths she buried deep.

He saw the darkness
and loved her
because of it.

Some men covet
to hold an angel in their midst,
but he wanted nothing more
than to touch the dark green witch
hiding behind her smile.

Heaven and Hell

There's something to be said

about the way he clings to her

calloused hands,

unshaven face,

buried into her skin.

Heaven, some would say.

But she knew

only the Devil

could feel

so delightfully

sinful.

A Million Times, Him

His lips grazed hers softly
as though asking a question.

His eyes implored her for the answer
she did not quickly give
not because she didn't know it,
but because
she wasn't prepared
for what it meant.

She never wanted to kiss another
in her lifetime

but him...

a million times,
him.

For All Seasons

She said to him,

"You are the warmth of the summer sun
lighting the path
to all my hopes and dreams.

You comfort me,
like the scent of fresh-cut grass
on a cool spring day.

You blanket me in security,
like snow falling
from a winter sky.

My love for you
is deeply rooted —
like the tallest trees in fall.

You are my love
for all seasons,

and all time."

When Love Spoke Aloud

They were connected, those two

and like poets and dreamers before them,

they wrote about it,

spoke about it,

sang it from the rooftops.

It often left others flustered

uneasy at their need

to speak their love so openly.

But it didn't bother them.

They only wondered

when love

had become

so silent

for everyone else.

Soul to Soul

She could feel him in everything now

his energy,

his laugh,

his love

running deeply through her.

He was the moon above her,

the ground beneath her feet.

He was in her walk,

in her words

as if some old-world magic

had bound them,

not just hand in hand,

but

soul to soul.

Infinite

She wanted a love that was over the top

a writer,

a dreamer,

a man who knew a thousand ways

to say I love you

without ever saying it the same way twice.

She wanted to read his words

again and again,

and still feel

that first-time rush.

She had spent her whole life

longing to be infinite

and in the words of a poet,

she always would be.

….. She was unapologetically herself.

No longer caring what people thought,

or what people say.

She put on her witch's hat,

and she wore it proudly …..

The Balance Beam

Life is just one long balance beam.

You stand in the middle,
hoping to keep your world from tilting

and yet,
standing there
in the safety of the center,

life simply passes you
idly by.

A Chance to Begin Again

In the stillness of the morning,
the sun warm upon my face
amazing what a year can do,
unbelievable what it can erase.

Broken out of the cage
that once held me within,
free from the bars that bound me
my wings, finally healed.

Mentally, I still flounder
as I glide through brighter skies.
Time can't heal everything
some damage will always be mine.

But I face each day headfirst,
taking off into the wind
and really, who could ask for more
than a chance
to begin again?

Morning Magic

She loves mornings

the sun beaming warm upon her face,

some old Motown jam

spinning through the radio,

and a cup of coffee

steady in her hand,

fueling her soul.

The Girl I Am Now

I don't know who I love more —

the girl I am now,

or the one I pretended to be

for so long.

Or maybe

it's the fact

that most days,

I no longer know

which is which.

The Girl Who Isn't Afraid Anymore

She is no stranger to loss.

That girl had it all

and lost it all.

She's walked barefoot on rock bottom,

climbed mountains

with bloodied knuckles and open hands.

A girl like her

isn't scared of anything anymore.

She doesn't flinch at endings

she thrives

on new beginnings.

Fall and Rise

She is fall leaves, tumbling to the ground
not because she is weak,
but because falling
was always part of her plan.

There she will break apart,
her brittle pieces rooting deep,
growing into something new
come spring.

You see
she may fall a million times,
but she will rise
a million more.

On Fire About Something

She is feisty.

Unapologetic.

Unforgiving.

Laughing and smiling

through the chaos —

leaving you reeling

in her wake.

She scorches the ground

as she walks,

and leaves them wondering

what could be

so worth

being on fire about.

The Making of Her

It's not that the mold was broken
when she was made

it's that she is
all the broken pieces
of her life's lessons,

coarsely stitched back together
to make something
terrifyingly new.

A woman
who has survived
it all.

......and so, the Witch

lived happily

and magically

Ever After!

Child of the Earth

The wind wears my name

in a language older than time.

I hear it echo

from the mountains,

carried

on eagles' wings as they fly.

I am a child of the Earth

a goddess aligned with the sun.

I walk in balance

with the elements,

as though

I am the only one.

Selective Caring

I used to beg — despairingly —
for the bare minimum.

Now I won't settle for less
than the space-time continuum.

My caring is selective;
I typically pick and choose.

I love the people I love
the rest, I'm content to lose.

Perhaps it seems disheartening
to those who care to stay,

but the people I have lost
simply moved
out of the way.

The Raven Returns

Soundless wings, black as night,

leap from trees and take to flight.

Moon on feathers, stars in eyes

gracefully soaring through darkened skies.

Beak on a window, let me in.

I've come to cleanse you of your sin.

Scavengers stirring in the dead of night,

waiting to bring your fears to light.

Tales of the Moon

Tiny sliver of a moon,
nestled above burnt orange hues.

I whisper my secrets with a laugh
she listens intently,
says nothing back.

I wonder if she's lonely up there,
among the clamor of starry fare.

She grows full of stories
until she can hold no more,

then disappears monthly
to let the weight outpour.

They fall from her
into the night sky,

becoming the stars
only clouds can hide.

The Blessing of Age

Sunlight dances across her face,

accentuating the laugh lines

that trace a path beneath her eyes.

Silver threads glimmer in her hair

as she breathes in

the newness of morning.

She is truly

who she was always meant to be

more at peace

than she ever dreamed she'd find.

Getting older,

she's come to see,

is the truest

kind of blessing.

The Locked Door

There's a locked door
along a wooded path
it sits in the middle of nowhere,
yet somehow
exactly where it's at.

They say, "Don't walk through it."
Instead, step aside.
Surely it stands here for a reason
it begs you
to come inside.

There is a key
buried deep within you.

Do you remember
how to find it there
or did you lose it
long ago,
when personal demons
silenced your care?

Witchery

There's a quiet in the night
that most would fear,
but the silence of the darkness
has always drawn her near.

There's something about that woman
others can't resist

magic dances in her eyes,
and witchery
paints her lips.

Stories of the Moon

I like it when the moon is bright,
illuminating all within my sight.

I also love when the moon is dark,
when the world feels dull
and lacking spark.

Perhaps that's why
I like people the same
shining brightly,
or quiet and plain.

Full of stories
and lessons on life,
or barely breathing,
heavy with strife.

We all have tales
we dare not tell,
while others spill theirs
from a verbal well.

Try and Come for Me

Gone was the girl who hid in the shadows,
unsure of what would come.
Gone was the girl who masked her strength,
always on the verge of coming undone.
She never wanted to carry a title
once content to simply blend.
But now she stood, bare before them,
her brazen magic and beauty shining in her grin.

There was a time they would have come for her
dragged her out, burned her at the stake.
But now she was queen on a throne of her own;
she had no patience for liars, fools, or fakes.
She stood before the mirror and adjusted her crown
a black, pointed witch's hat for the world to see.
Then she painted her door purple, sat on her porch,
and dared them

"Try and come for me."

All Women Are Witches

The word Witch has followed me through life sometimes whispered, sometimes spat, but always present. Once, it was meant to wound me. Now, it crowns me. I wear it not as a mark of religion, but as a symbol of reclamation. The word Witch belongs to every woman who has ever been told to be quiet, to shrink, to stay small. You don't have to practice magic to feel her power; you only have to remember your own.

In these pages, I speak often of the word Witch; a word that has been twisted, feared, and used to burn women for the simple act of being powerful. I ask you now to reclaim it.

For lifetimes, women have been judged, silenced, shunned, and even killed for daring to stand against the mold of society. I wear the word Witch as my rebellion against that conformity. It is not a curse; it is a crown.

To be a witch is to be a woman who refuses to bow. It is to be loud when the world demands quiet. It is to stand in your power, to speak your truth, to let your fire burn and your roots grow deep.

No matter your faith or path, being a witch means you will not be tamed. It means you rise when others would have you fall. It means you choose to walk against the tide and dance while doing it.

We are not delicate things meant to be contained. We are the storm, the spark, the silence after lightning. We are beautiful. We are strong. We are a force to be reckoned with.

So put on your witch's hat, stand tall, and dare them to come for you, too

Acknowledgments

To my husband, Clay, my greatest cheerleader and steadfast anchor. Without your constant love, support, and encouragement, this book might have stayed locked away for another five years. Your unwavering belief in the beauty of my words gave me the courage to finally bring them into the light. I am forever grateful for you and all the ways you've helped me make this dream a reality.

To my children; thank you for loving me through every phase of my journey, unrelenting and true. For two decades you've wandered spiritual shops with me, walked through old cemeteries, and listened patiently to my endless tarot revelations. All the while, you've each carved your own paths with open hearts and curious spirits. It fills me with joy to see you honor nature and find beauty in all things. You six make me proud every single day.

And finally, a special thank you to Sydney Sidon of 7 Feathers Photography, for capturing my inner witch just in time for my back cover photo. Your artistry brought the magic to life all the mystical, powerful vibes this book deserved.

Coming 2026

Blacklisted: A Survival Story Told Through Poetry and Prose

Before there was light, there was the darkness that tried to bury her.

Before there was magic, there was the girl who had forgotten her own name.

Blacklisted is the story of a woman who gave everything, her youth, her voice, her soul, to a love that became a prison.

It is a journey through fear, silence, and betrayal; through addiction, violence, and survival.

It is the voice of a mother who fought back, the woman who ran, and the witch who rose.

Told through raw poetry and prose, this collection is not just a story of escape, it's a resurrection.

About the Author

Shel Chrisco's journey with poetry began in Mrs. Brink's English class, where she first met the words of Poe, Whitman, Plath, and Shakespeare. Encouraged by her teacher to enter her early poems into contests, one of which was published, Shel discovered that poetry wasn't just something she loved; it was part of who she was.

Today, Shel is a poet, farmer, and modern "witch" whose work bridges the seen and unseen worlds. Her debut collection, The Purple Door: A Spiritual Journey Through Poetry and Prose, traces a transformative path through darkness, magic, and rebirth. Inspired by her life on Vulture and Raven Hollow, her family's farm, her writing is steeped in nature's rhythm, ancestral whispers, and the balance between light and shadow.

When she isn't writing beneath the moon, being a wife, mother, and "NayNay," Shel tends her animals and shares her poetry and musings as @shelchriscopoetry on social media and at www.shelchriscopoetry.com , inviting others to explore their own wild, sacred selves.